730

MG TF

Jonathan Edwards

CONTENTS

Foulis

Haynes

ISBN 0 85429 382 5

A FOULIS Motoring Book

First published 1984

© **Haynes Publishing Group**

Published by:
Haynes Publishing Group
Sparkford, Yeovil,
Somerset BA22 7JJ

Haynes Publications Inc.
861 Lawrence Drive, Newbury
Park, California 91320, USA

**British Library Cataloguing in
Publication Data**
Edwards, Jonathan
  MG TF super profile
  1. M.G. automobile
  I. Title
  629.2'222 TL215.M2
  ISBN 0-85429-382-5

Dust jacket design: Rowland Smith
Jacket colour illustration: The MG
TF1250 of John Haynes,
photographed by Les Brazier
Page Layout: Mike King
Photographs: Andrew Morland,
Les Brazier
Road test: Courtesy of *Motor*
Printed in England by:
J.H. Haynes & Co. Ltd

Titles in the *Super Profile* series

Ariel Square Four (F388)
BMW R69 & R69S (F387)
Brough Superior SS100 (F364)
BSA A7 & A10 (F446)
BSA Bantam (F333)
Honda CB750 sohc (F351)
Matchless G3L & G80 (F455)
MV Agusta America (F334)
Norton Commando (F335)
Sunbeam S7 & S8 (F363)
Triumph Thunderbird (F353)
Triumph Trident (F352)
Triumph Bonneville (F453)
Velocette KSS (F444)
*Vincent B & C Series Twins
(F460)*
AC/Ford/Shelby Cobra (F381)
*Austin-Healey 'Frogeye' Sprite
(F343)*
Chevrolet Corvette (F432)
Ferrari 250GTO (F308)
Fiat X1/9 (F341)
Ford Cortina 1600E (F310)
Ford GT40 (F332)
Jaguar E-Type (F370)
Jaguar D-Type & XKSS (F371)
Jaguar Mk 2 Saloons (F307)
Jaguar SS90 & SS100 (F372)
Lancia Stratos (F340)
Lotus Elan (F330)
Lotus Seven (F385)
MGB (F305)
*MG Midget & Austin-Healey
Sprite (except 'Frogeye')
(F344)*
Mini Cooper (F445)
Morris Minor Series MM (F412)
*Morris Minor & 1000 (ohv)
(F331)*
Porsche 911 Carrera (F311)
Rolls-Royce Corniche (F411)
Triumph Stag (F342)

Bell U-H1 (F437)
B29 Superfortress (F339)
Boeing 707 (F356)
Grumman F8F Bearcat (F447)
Harrier (F357)
Hawker Hunter (F448)
MIG 21 (F439)
Mosquito (F422)
Phantom II (F376)
P51 Mustang (F423)
Sea King (F377)
SEPECAT Jaguar (F438)
Super Etendard (F378)
Tiger Moth (F421)
Vulcan (F436)

Great Western Kings (F426)
Intercity 125 (F428)
V2 'Green Arrow' Class (F427)

FOREWORD

The MG TF has always been a controversial car. When it was new, some criticised it for looking old-fashioned, while others loved it for precisely the same reason. MG's designers themselves would rather not have had to produce it at all, for they wanted to develop a more modern prototype instead. Now, in the 1980s, the supply of top-quality TFs is limited, the cost of restoration is high, and values seem to have gone through the roof. The type, indeed, is so popular – or should I say 'fashionable'? – that several very authentic-looking replicas have been put on sale, at least one of them utilising a rear-engined VW Beetle chassis!

Let me make my position clear right from the start. I am old enough to have known the TF when it was a production car, young enough to see that in some ways it has not stood the test of time, but enough of a romantic to love its looks, its handling characteristics and its 'Abingdon-built' character. I have always thought the TF to be the nicest of all the classic T-Series MGs, though I have always been disappointed by its lack of performance compared with its rivals. Way back in 1953, I could not see how MG (or, in fairness, their owners at BMC, whose idea it was) had the nerve to launch the traditional-style MG TF in the face of stiff competition from the Triumph TR2 and the Austin-Healey 100. Even today, when the car's reputation is probably at its peak, I am still amazed that they seemed to get away with it – albeit for less than two years.

The story of the MG TF is not simple, for it involves a great deal of fudging, corporate skullduggery and cynical marketing on the part of the British Motor Corporation. This group had been founded in 1952, the marriage of the Nuffield Organisation with Austin, and even by the end of the first year the new supremo, Leonard Lord, had started a far-reaching rationalisation and 'badge-engineering' programme.

If Nuffield had not merged with Austin, they might have approved production of Syd Enever's EX175 project and what we know now as the MGA might have been on the market much earlier. In that scenario, therefore, the T-Series would have died with the TD, and the TF might never have been born. But Leonard Lord, his agreement with Donald Healey over the Healey 100 project and his long-held antipathy to all-things Nuffield blocked out EX175 for two long years and something – the TF – had to take its place. The miracle is that with such a limited time to make a 'different' model out of the TF, John Thornley and Syd Enever managed to produce an interim car of which 9,600 were eventually sold.

I hope, therefore, that this Super Profile will put the life and times of the TF firmly into perspective. I have had the advantage, over other British researchers at least, in being given access to the actual Abingdon chassis production ledgers which tell in graphic detail how the car got off to a fine start but began to run down early in 1955. Also, I have to admit, I have the benefit of hindsight – but this has not altered my overall impression of the car one bit. It was a fine car when new, and it is a classic today.

To prepare this volume, I drew on 30 years of involvement in the motoring, and motoring-writing business but I would also like to thank those who helped me enormously in the project :

To Peter Mitchell and Anders Clausager, of BL Heritage, who provided research facilities and the opportunity to study the MG TF production records, which they hold.

Bernard Jesty of Weymouth, not only for talking about his car but for letting us photograph it on a very dusty Dorset day!

John Haynes, chairman of the Haynes Publishing Company, for providing 'the other' TF pictured in these pages.

Roche Bentley, the organising genius behind the MG Owners Club, for putting me in touch with TF enthusiasts, and Richard Monk of the same club who provided a selection of T-Series colour photographs.

Bryan Kennedy of Connoisseur Carbooks – he knows why!

Tony Stafford, one of the UK's many TF enthusiasts, for talking about his car.

Thanks also go to *Motor,* for their permission to print original technical and road test material.

– and, of course, to Andrew Morland and Les Brazier, for their diligence over photography, without which my words would mean so little.

HISTORY

When the MG TF was launched in October 1953, just before the opening of the British Earls Court Motor Show, it produced many reactions from sports car enthusiasts all round the world — surprise, pleasure, disappointment, amazement and relief all among them. Looking back, it is obvious why this should be so — for the TF was a traditionally-styled MG, revealed at a time when sleekly-styled rival products were appearing on all sides. The TF, like its ancestors, retained separate, sweeping, front wings, running boards, and an upright radiator grille. It was controversial then, and has been controversial ever since.

Even so, it would be truer to say that the TF was, at best, a 'second choice' car from MG's management, who would much rather have pressed ahead with a modern, beautifully-styled, project called EX175, which we now know as the MGA. Their financial masters at BMC, in Birmingham, however, gave this car the thumbs-down at the time and the TF had to be produced in a tearing hurry. Having announced the TF, MG clearly had to believe in it as best they could but they were obviously half-hearted about attempts to improve it further. It was a model produced for less than two years, it did not sell as well as its predecessor, the

TD, and there was much criticism of it in the specialist press.

However, although it became fashionable in later years to denigrate the TF as a failure it was definitely not that, for it sold faster than any previous MG model except the TD. Now, in the era of 'classic' sports cars, the TF is often described as the most attractive of all the 'traditional' MGs.

Midget Ancestry

As to its ancestors; these I ought to summarise, right from the start. The TF's direct ancestor, having almost exactly the same rolling chassis, was the TD of 1950-1953, but there were also direct and important family connections all the way back to the original T-Series model, the TA of 1936, with visual and philosophical links to the very first Midget, the M-series of 1928. The traditional MG style and mechanical layout once established at the end of the 1920s, was very strong — you only have to compare an M-Series, a J2, a PB, a TA and a TF to see this proved.

The very first MG-badged cars were built in 1924, in a business owned personally by William Morris (later Lord Nuffield) but inspired by Cecil Kimber. The name MG stood for 'Morris Garages', Morris's own Oxford-based garage business where Kimber was at first employed. Steady expansion led to sports car design and assembly being centred on a factory at Abingdon, just south of Oxford — then in Berkshire, but since 1970's boundary changes officially in Oxfordshire — the first car to be built in large numbers being the 847cc-engined M-Series Midget.

By 1935 the MG sports car range was complex, growing ever-more expensive, but selling less and less well than in the early 1930s and — unhappily — making financial losses for Lord Nuffield (who, in

fairness, could well afford to stand this loss). In that year, he allowed the Morris Motors managing director, an abrasive character called Leonard Lord, to complete a sweeping reorganisation, part of which involved the MG Car Co. (his own personal business) being transferred into corporate ownership under Morris Motors, as part of the new Nuffield organisation. Leonard Lord then swept through the business like a tornado, closed down the design departments and the motor racing activities, sentenced the special overhead-camshaft models to death, and ordered Nuffield to design a new series of cars using Morris-based running gear.

The result of this sweeping policy change was not only the launch of three new saloon MGs — the SA, VA and WA types — but a new two-seater sports car, the T-Series (which only became known as the TA after it had been superseded), which used modified Morris Ten/Wolseley 10 engine, gearbox and final drive. The chassis had beam front and rear axles, sprung on rock-hard half-elliptic leaf springs, while the body style was much as before with flowing wings, a vertical radiator, separate headlamps and a shell built up on the basis of a wooden (ash) skeleton by the Morris Bodies Branch in Coventry.

In less than three years a total of 3003 TAs were built, then in 1939 the car was re-engined to become the TB, of which only 379 cars were built before the outbreak of the Second World War. The engine and the gearbox were both important to the TF of 1953, for they would be used in modified form for that car. The engine design was all-new, from the Morris Engines branch, and featured simple but robust construction, pushrod overhead valve gear and cast iron cylinder block and head castings. It was originally fitted to the technically-advanced Morris 10 Series M (the first Nuffield product to have a unit construction body/chassis unit), when its swept volume was 1140cc and its peak power (aided by the use of a single SU Carburettor) was 37 bhp.

Coded as XPJM, this unit was also adopted for the Wolseley 10 of 1939, but for the TB it was supertuned in the same way that the old long-stroke TA engine had been, given larger cylinder bores, a capacity of 1250cc and peak power of 54 bhp at 5200 rpm. The new XPAG unit was an altogether better engine than the one it replaced — smaller, lighter, better-breathing, and stronger — and the future would show that it was quite amazingly tuneable, something which MG engineers could not have known when they saw the engine imposed upon them (for such, indeed it was) in 1939.

Post-war Development

After the Second World War, the TB became the TC. Mechanically almost unchanged but with a slightly widened body, 10,000 of these cars were built from 1945 to 1949. More importantly, a total of 2001 were exported to the USA, thus establishing an MG foothold in the North American continent which would become so important to them in future years.

In the meantime, Nuffield had also introduced two new models — the Y-Series saloon, and the YT Tourer evolved from it. The Y-Series chassis, designed before the Second World War and originally intended for launch in 1940, featured box section side members, and independent front suspension by coil springs and transverse wishbones, the top 'wishbone' actually being formed by the arms of the hydraulic lever-arm shock absorbers fixed to the cross-member, while motive power was by a detuned version of the XPAG engine. This chassis, and its front suspension, were to be very important to the development of the TF in 1953.

Next on the scene at Abingdon came the TD sports car, needed to replace the TC which, although selling better than any previous MG model, was beginning to be seen as out of date. Immediately after the war, when any new car was snapped up by eager buyers, this did not matter. Now, in 1949, mere newness was no longer enough.

Faced with the need to produce a successor to the TC, not only in a great hurry but with virtually no development budget, John Thornley, Syd Enever, Alec Hounslow and their colleagues looked to the Y-Series chassis for a solution. Their first effort of 1949 was, quite literally, to shorten the wheelbase of a Y-Series frame, from 8ft 3in, to 7ft 10in, plonk an existing TC body shell on to this, carve it about as necessary, and assess the results.

It might not have been pretty (no pictures survive, it seems), but it proved to be very promising and it led to a proper 7ft 10in frame being designed, and a squatter, more suitable, body shell being evolved to cover the wider wheel tracks of the chassis layout. The frame produced for the new car, which became the TD, was not simply a shortened Y-Series, however, as it had side members, overslung of the rear axle, rather than underslung as in the Y-Series, while for the TD there was a new type of hypoid bevel back axle, where the existing Y-Series saloons still used a Nuffield spiral bevel design. The body shell for the TD, based, as ever, on a wooden skeleton, was produced on very simple jigging and tooling by the Morris Bodies Branch factory in Coventry, while the frame was bought in from an outside supplier.

The first TDs were built in November 1949, the car was revealed to the public in January 1950, and for the next four years it sold very well indeed, breaking all previous Abingdon output records. It was the first MG sports car ever built with the option of left-hand

steering, which made it doubly attractive to the North American market, while the supple independent front suspension, allied to rack and pinion steering, made the ride and handling acceptable at last.

Time, however, was marching on, sports car fashions were changing and there were corporate upheavals in the air. For the MG Car Co. Ltd, 1952 was a complete watershed; not only was this the year in which the Nuffield Organisation formally merged with Austin (to form the new British Motor Corporation), but it was also the year in which prototypes of the Austin-Healey 100 and the Triumph TR2, were unveiled.

The arrival of the Austin-Healey and Triumph models, complete with attractive full-width body styling and all-steel coachwork, signalled the obsolescence of the TD, but at the Earls Court Motor Show of that year MG had nothing new to display in reply.

It was not a situation of their own choosing, for a tiny development team, led by Syd Enever and aided and abetted by John Thornley wherever possible, had already decided how the TD should be replaced. In 1951, MG had provided a startlingly attractive new body shell for George Phillips' MG TD chassis, to compete at Le Mans. However, this hybrid resulted in the driver having to sit rather high, so in 1952, with no formal development budget behind him, Enever decided to do something about this. Under project code EX175, he designed a completely new, much lower chassis which had wider-spaced side members to pick up the TD's front suspension and steering, and which would use the existing engine and transmission. One frame was used in a record car (EX179) not built until 1954, but the other went into a complete prototype road car, which MG then submitted to BMC's chairman, Leonard Lord, for approval as a future production car to replace the TD.

Unfortunately for them, Lord had already decided to back the Healey 100 project, renaming it *Austin*-Healey 100 and having it assembled at Longbridge, and was in no mood to approve what promised to be a rival to it. MG, he said, would have to soldier on with the TD, which was still at the peak of its popularity; in 1952, nearly 11,000 TDs would be produced, the vast majority being destined for sale in the United States.

Thornley and Enever were stunned by this rejection of their EX175 prototype, but did not scrap it, merely putting it aside, sure in their belief that it would be needed, and approved, one day. For the time being, therefore, they carried on building the TD — only to find, within months, that sales were beginning to drop away rapidly. It was not an immediate and catastrophic slump in demand, but it was consistent — as the TD moved into its fourth year of production, still looking exactly as it had in 1950, sports car buffs in North America, who liked novelty, began to turn away looking for something new.

BMC's boss, Leonard Lord, would not sanction a radically new model, but he did, at least, allow MG to do something — which was to produce a face-lift on the TD. Logically, according to the way all previous MGs had been titled, such a face lift should have become the TE, but Tee-Hee sounded similar and somehow it wasn't dignified enough. So, TF it was, and as rapidly as possible; there never was a TE, not even a prototype.

There was neither time, nor tooling capital, available to develop a new chassis or running gear, so it was decided to use, virtually unchanged, the existing TD's mechanical equipment, and to concentrate all efforts on the body shell. Even in this case, however, the basic centre section of the TD, cutaway doors and all, had to be retained, the changes having to be concentrated on the nose and the tail.

TD Metamorphosis — the TF

We now know, from interviews given by John Thornley and by Cec Cousins (MG's works director at the time), that the 'restyle' was no more than a co-operative effort between Alec Hounslow, Enever and Cousins, with the aid of a resourceful 'tin-basher' (sheet metal worker) called Billy Wilkins. There was no question of drawings being made at first — the TF prototype took shape 'in the metal' as work progressed. First the existing TD radiator was leaned back a little to make the car look somewhat less severe (but this was only temporary, for production TFs had a rather more contoured radiator style), and this allowed the bonnet line to be dipped sharply towards the nose, the reduction in height actually being more than three inches.

Next the front wings were reshaped, more or less by eye, with the headlamps being partly recessed into pods, for the first time on an MG. Another change, for cheapness rather than for ease of access, was that the bonnet sides became fixed and only the top of the bonnet could be hinged up so that the engine could be worked on.

At the rear, the wings were reshaped to give a more rakish aspect, with a new rake to the fuel tank being angled to suit. In the centre section, whose 'skeleton' was essentially unchanged, there was still a folding windscreen, but the wiper mechanism was now concealed under the bodywork.

The most obvious change in the cockpit was a new facia with a padded crash roll, in which octagonally-shaped instruments were placed in a centrally-positioned panel common both to left-hand and right-hand drive cars. (On the TD, the speedometer and rev counter were positioned one side or the other to suit the steering wheel position).

The prototype, given a chassis number of 0250, though officially it was TD 3/26849 (which confirms its provenance) was on the road in May 1953. Alec Hounslow states that it was left outside John Thornley's office for him to approve when he got back to work after a short holiday, and that all the proving work it had done was to be driven 'to Marcham and back'. [Since Marcham is all of two miles from the Abingdon factory, that cannot have taken very long!] He also recalls that after Thornley had approved it, and directed that the TF should be in production before the 1953 Earls Court Motor Show (to be held in October), the prototype then had to be handed over to the drawing office to be officially 'designed' and drawn up!

Of course, there were some significant, if not startling, changes to the running gear. The most obvious visible improvement was that centre-lock wire-spoke wheels were optional to the standard perforated discs. These wheels, in fact, had become optional late in the life of the TD (according to the official Parts Lists, that is to say, though I have never yet seen a wire-wheel equipped TD straight out of the factory).

The XPAG engine was still the familiar 1250cc unit, but it received many of the 'Mk II' tuning modifications as standard, had small pancake air cleaners, rather than trunking to a remote cleaner, and peak output was quoted at 57 bhp (net) at 5,500 rpm. The final drive ratio was raised from the 5.125:1 of the TD to 4.875:1, while the gearbox itself was not altered.

In some ways the TF had advanced, but in others it had regressed. There were individually adjustable seats (the TF had had a bench squab), and there were flashing direction indicators for all markets (the TD used these for some markets, but not all). On the other hand, there was still no fuel gauge, while the TF became the first Midget to sport a dummy radiator grille, topped by a dummy water radiator cap.

The first, and only, official TF 'pre-production' car (it still exists) was built on 12 August, given a chassis number of 0251, but also carried TD2/29748. This car, in fact, took shape amid the last flood of TDs, for TDs were assembled until 17 August, and the last of their chassis numbers was TD2/29915.

Series production of TFs got under way immediately after the last TDs had been built, the biggest delay no doubt being at the Morris Bodies Branch in Coventry, where the revised body panels and jigging had to be installed. At Abingdon, in fact, there was a two week hiatus, for the first nine production TFs were started on 3 September 1953 (the chassis build records still exist, and are held by BL Heritage), and the first two cars were not completed until 16 September. Three more were finished off on 17 September, a further five on 18 September, after which the build up was rapid.

As every MG enthusiast knows, previous Midgets had started their production life at Chassis No. 0251 (251 was MG's Abingdon telephone number – isn't that romantic!), but in 1953 BMC were having no more of that nonsense. Like other BMC cars of the day, it was decreed that production should begin at 0501 instead, and so it was – 0501, started on 3 September, was a black car with red trim and disc wheels.

The original production sanction (approval to order a certain number of components) was for 7000 cars, which on previous TD experience would not keep the assembly lines going for more than nine months or so. Once established, production built up quickly, the 1000th TF production car being completed on 7 December 1953, just two months after the model had been revealed

to the world. At this point, the 'take' of optional wire spoke wheels was about 50 per cent (it actually increased, as time passed) and the vast majority of all the early cars were in left-hand drive, destined for export to the United States. By the turn of the year, 40 TFs were being completed every day – equivalent to production of about 200/week or 10,000/year, which would almost have matched the achievement of the TD had production been maintained.

But there were problems. The TF was received coolly by the press, if only because it was rather overshadowed by Gerald Palmer's elegant four-door saloon with BMC B-Series running gear, called the MG ZA Magnette, also to be assembled at Abingdon (though not ready, in fact, until the very end of 1953). Both the Austin-Healey 100 (at a UK basic price of £750) and the 2.0-litre Triumph TR2 (£555) were already available, which did not make the traditional-looking TF appear a bargain at £550.

Perhaps, however, resistance to the styling and in particular the limited performance (the TF's top speed of 80 mph compared very badly with the 100 + gait of the TR2, for instance) has been over-stated by historians in recent years, for the TF began to sell well, if not sensationally well. More than 3000 cars had been built before the end of February 1954, by which time two in every three cars were being assembled with wire spoke wheels.

Although optional final drive ratios and 'stage' engine tuning were still available, the records show very little call for this sort of gear; the first such 'special', with a

4.55:1 axle and a tuned engine, was built on 1 March 1954 for a home market customer, and another example followed five weeks later.

Even in the spring of 1954, the spirit was strong at Abingdon. The sanction was increased to 10,000 cars in February, and the 5,000th TF was completed on 12 May, just seven months after launch. But all this hid the worrying news coming back from the USA, where disappointment with the car's looks and its performance, was filtering back; behind the scenes, MG engineers were already rushing to do something about this.

Perhaps if the TF had been enjoying any successful type of competition career, sales might have been helped, but in 1954 there was little call for this. The balance and the general roadholding abilities of the TF were as good as that of any other car (it was, for instance, particularly suited to driving tests, or gymkhanas, where compact size, direct steering, and the fly-off handbrake all helped considerably), but it quite simply lacked straight-line performance. It really was no good die-hard MG enthusiasts scoffing about the TR2's roadholding, or the Big Healey's lack of ground clearance, for both these cars could blow off the TF in almost any sporting contest.

Perhaps it was a little suspicious that BMC did not allow any British motoring magazine to test the TF, even if the USA's *Road & Track* magazine had headed their test of March 1954, 'America's Best Sports Car Buy', when the TF 1250 was priced at $2260, FOB East Coast. Indeed, they opened their text by stating: "Of all the cars which we have occasion to drive there is one above all others which, by its every characteristic, clearly defines the term 'sports car'." They saw past the styling, and dug deep, to get to know the TF's endearing character: "To drive an MG is sheer pleasure. This is no car for the average Joe looking for transportation. Only those who know and appreciate the fun of driving a car which responds to skilful handling will ever get to like an MG... the fact remains that the entire staff of *Road & Track* vied with each other to produce the best reason for using the MG."

For BMC, that was the good news, but the bad news was contained in comments that "the new TF is an anomaly — a retrogression. The revised styling, though lower and more rakish, is still far from being modern. The performance is well below the 1954 Detroit norm..." Here at home, *Autosport,* thought that:

"the TF is... built for the non-competition-minded class of purchaser, which, it must be admitted, forms the bulk of the small-capacity sports car users", which smacks of damning by faint praise.

Something, it was clear, would have to be done. Fortunately for MG, something was already being done, and in the summer of

1954, it became apparent on the assembly lines at Abingdon. After the TF1250, the TF1500 was already on the way.

EVOLUTION

As I have already made clear, the MG TF was only ever intended to be a stop-gap model, something to keep the T-Series pot boiling until John Thornley could persuade BMC that he should be allowed to put an entirely new sports car (the MGA) into production. There is ample evidence to suggest that MG never really planned further changes to the TF after it had been released, though the development of the enlarged XPEG type of engine must have been under way by that time. Accordingly, apart from the arrival of the TF 1500 derivative in the summer of 1954, there are no other important development changes to report.

I ought to make one point about the TF1250 very clear. Although many historians have quoted motoring writers' comments, to the effect that the TF was a disappointment, and that this helped MG to convince BMC that it should be ditched as soon as possible, the fact was that it still sold well and must have made money for the company. It did not sell as well as the TD, of which 10,838 cars were built in 1952, but in 1954 (the only calendar year in which the TF was being built from start to finish), 6,520 cars were built, which was better than any other MG model apart from the TD. So, please, don't condemn it out of hand.

There was no hiding the TF's limitations, however. It was obvious to almost everyone that it was no more than a face-lifted TD, and by comparison with the new 2.0-litre Triumph TR2 (itself no runaway sales success at first, let's not forget) it was neither modern-looking, economical nor fast enough.

Something had to be done. Early in 1954, when a disappointing response to the car had become obvious (particularly in the USA, where the vast majority of deliveries were being made), there was no question of doing yet another body restyle, and this meant that the car would always have to live with appallingly bluff aerodynamics, and a poor top speed.

Nor could it be made lighter, and therefore more accelerative, without making it much more expensive. A slimmed-down chassis frame would not be as stiff as before, and roadholding would suffer, while aluminium body panels would never save enough weight to justify their extra material costs.

The only practical improvement was to provide more power, and to make the car more lively than before, for independent road test figures showed that the existing TF accelerated no better than the TD of 1950-1953 had always done. Perhaps an engine transplant (from the new ZA Magnette, which had the 1489cc BMC B-Series unit) was considered, under protest, but this would have entailed a different gearbox as well, and probably too much complication. Instead, MG decided to look at ways of squeezing more power out of the existing engine.

It could be done in two ways – either by super-tuning (which, effectively, meant dipping into the store of experience built up with 'stage' tuning for competition TCs and TDs), or by enlarging the unit. Super-tuning would have produced a less flexible, less 'roadable'

engine, so enlarging the unit was the only answer.

The XP series, however, had never been designed with a great deal of 'stretch' in its cylinder block. When revealed in 1938, as the XPJM, the Morris Motors unit had a bore and stroke of 63.5 x 90mm, and a capacity of 1140cc. For the TB of 1939, and all subsequent Midgets up to this point, the bore had been increased to 66.5mm, the capacity of 1250cc, and (in tuned form) the type number became XPAG. In the early 1950s, following the foundation of BMC, it was living on borrowed time, for it was not favoured for future use; this segment of Leonard Lord's master plan was to be covered by the newly-designed BMC B-Series unit.

There was, however, some scope for enlargement. By arranging to siamese pairs of cylinders, but by keeping the same basic casting wall thicknesses, Morris Engines branch produced a re-cored cylinder block and new machined cylinder bores of 72mm, which allowed a swept volume of 1466cc. Supplies were to be made available to MG as soon as possible, but to prove the point the all-new MG record car, EX179, was given a super-tuned version of the unit. Type XPEG, as it was called (where the 'E' stood for 'Enlarged', if it stood for anything at all!), looked exactly like the XPAG from the outside, as the main casting dimensions, cylinder centres, cylinder head, carburettors and manifolds were all unchanged. The 17 per cent cubic capacity increase achieved resulted in 10 per cent more peak power, and 17 per cent more torque, which was all predictable. Comparative figures were:

Model	Peak power	Peak torque
TF1250	57 bhp @ 5500 rpm	65 lb ft @ 3000 rpm
TF1500	63 bhp @ 5000 rpm	76 lb ft @ 3000 rpm

Chassis Nos.	Engines fitted	Final assembly dates
501 to 6500	XPAG, 1250cc	16 Sept 1953 to 14 July 1954
6501 to 6650	XPEG, 1466cc	21 July 1954 to 26 Aug 1954
6651 to 6750	XPAG, 1250cc	10 Aug 1954 to 26 Aug 1954
6751 to 6850	XPEG, 1466cc	26 Aug 1954 to 10 Sept 1954
6851 to 6950	XPAG, 1250cc	26 Aug 1954 to 22 Sept 1954
6951 onward	XPEG, 1466cc	From 10 Sept 1954

Unfortunately for posterity, MG did not make a clean change from the use of 1250cc to 1466cc engines on the assembly lines at Abingdon, for there was a period from Chassis No. 6500 to 6950 when both units were being used in batches. The details are given in the accompanying table.

The table shows not only that the changeover was statistically messy, with cars of different engine sizes being built in batches over a period of two months, but chronologically messy too, for there must have been times in August and September 1954 when cars with each engine size were being completed alongside (or behind) each other, on the same assembly lines! Complicated...

The introduction of the larger, more powerful, engine (only identified on the later cars by a small medallion on the sides of the bonnet) gave the TF a short-lived boost, but supplies did not reach the United States until early autumn, by which time the peak buying season was already over, so the sales impact was limited. Incidentally, although limited numbers of TF1500s were sold in the UK, the bigger engine was never advertised strongly and some export territories such as Australia and Canada never received TF 1500s at all.

Even before the TF1500 came into production at Abingdon, MG had been given the go-ahead to produce an all-new car, which they coded EX182, and which became the MGA in 1955, so no further development work was done on the TF. The car's first anniversary as a production car at Abingdon was celebrated on 16 September 1954, when cars in the Chassis Number range of around 7080 were being built (total assembly, therefore, being about 6,500 cars to this point).

The overall sanction had been increased, early in 1954, to 10,000 cars in total when about 200 cars were being completed every week, but this sanction was cut to 9,200, then restored to 9,600 in November 1954, and at the turn of the year assembly was at the rate of about 90 cars a week. Assembly of the final 1,000 cars began on 27 January 1955, and was completed on 12 April 1955 when the lines actually emptied.

At this time, in fact, everything was going wrong for MG and BMC, for they had hoped to replace the TF1500 by first supplies of the MGA sports car, but since supplies of pressed steel body shells (from Pressed Steel Co.!) were delayed, this was not possible. In fact, Abingdon did not build another sports car until August 1955 — four months later — the only cars being built throughout this time being MG Magnette and Riley Pathfinder saloons.

As with the TF1250, the Abingdon production records mention very few special TF1500s. A car-by-car analysis only turns up the few Motor Show cars (the 1954 Earls Court machines were Ch. Nos 7252 — Ivory with red trim — 7253 — Red with biscuit trim, for instance), while Ch. No. 9206 (Red with biscuit trim) was designated a 'Competition car', presumably that eventually registered KRX 90 and used by Pat Moss in the RAC International Rally, while 9417 was noted as having a 4.55:1 axle ratio and a tuned engine. As to those show cars, both were definitely 1466cc-engined machines, yet none of the British motoring magazines was given the information, and listed them as 1250s! Such was the dubious publicity expertise of the BMC in the 1950s.

In its 19 month life, therefore, the TF sold 9,600 examples, 3,400 of them with 1466cc engines, an average in round figures of 505 cars a month. This compares, say, with 645 cars a month for the TD, but only 196 TCs a month. and means that management must have been reasonably satisfied, if not overjoyed, with its career. However, almost every MG enthusiast agrees that MG would rather not have built the TF at all, if they could have had the MGA in 1953 instead.

TF Postscript

There were two ways in which the TF's heritage might have lived on, if certain people had got their way:

In 1952, when the MG's Syd Enever came to design a new low-slung chassis to complement the sleek body-style already produced for the 1951 TD-based Le Mans car, EX175 not only picked up the TD/TF's coil spring independent front suspension, but was given a TD1250 engine, gearbox and hypoid bevel axle. This car, registered HMO 6, needed a tiny bulge in its bonnet panel to accommodate the XPAG-type engine, and was offered for approval to Leonard Lord, just *after* the BMC chairman had decided to take over the Healey 100 design. By the time EX175 was resurrected in 1954 to replace the TF, MG were

instructed to use the B-Series power train from the Magnette saloon, and the car was recoded EX182.

In 1953, too, Gerald Palmer, who was Nuffield's chief designer and had already schemed out the new Magnette, proposed an interesting new body style on the basis of the TD/TF rolling chassis. This, he suggested, could be styled and assembled in two ways — as a traditional car, TD/TF style, for some markets, and as a more modern 'full-width' style for others, but it could still have used the same basic body 'core' with differing bolt-on wings and doors. This progressed as far as mock-up at the Nuffield styling studios at Cowley, but was never progressed any further.

SPECIFICATION

TF1250, produced 1953 and 1954

Type	TF sports car
Built	Abingdon, near Oxford
Numbers built	6,200
Drive configuration	Front engine, with gearbox mounted behind it, rear wheel drive.
Engine	BMC/Nuffield Type XPAG, Four cylinders, in line, conventionally mounted in fore-and-aft location. Cast iron cylinder block, with cast iron cylinder head. Two valves per cylinder, in line, operated by pushrods, and rockers from camshaft in side of block. Bore, stroke and capacity 66.5 x 90mm, 1250 cc (2.62 x 3.54in, 76.27 cu in); 8.0:1 compression ratio. Two semi-downdraught constant-vacuum SU H4 carburettors. Maximum power 57 bhp (net) at 5,500 rpm. Maximum torque 65 lb ft at 3,000 rpm.
Transmission	Four-speed gearbox, mounted immediately behind the engine, with synchromesh on top, third and second gears. Overall gearbox ratios 17.06, 10.09, 6.752, 4.875, reverse 17.06:1. Hypoid bevel final drive, ratio 4.875:1.
Chassis	Separate box-section chassis frame supporting all mechanical components, incorporating stiffening hoop ahead of facia panel. Wheelbase 7ft 10in (238.8cm) Track (front), 3ft 11.4in (120.3cm) with disc wheels; 4ft 0.19in (122.4 cm) with centre-lock wire wheels. Track (rear), 4ft 2in (127 cm) with disc wheels; 4ft 2.81in (129.0 cm) with centre-lock wire wheels.
Suspension	Front: Independent, by coil springs, lower wishbones, and upper wishbone arms incorporated in mechanism of hydraulic lever-arm dampers. No anti-roll bar. Rear: Live rear axle, by half-elliptic leaf springs, and hydraulic lever-arm dampers. No anti-roll bar.

Steering	Rack and pinion: 2.8 turns lock-to-lock
Brakes	Lockheed hydraulic, front and rear drums, with no vacuum servo assistance. Dimensions: 9.0 in. drum diameter, 1.5in. shoe width. Two-leading shoe operation at front, leading and trailing operation at rear. Mechanical handbrake operation by centrally mounted lever with 'fly-off' actuation.
Wheels and tyres	Standard equipment: pressed-steel perforated bolt-on disc wheels, with four-stud fixing; 15in rim diameter and 4.0in rim width; 5.50-15in cross-ply tyres. Optional centre-lock wire-spoke wheels; same rim diameter and width.
Bodywork	Traditional-style and traditional coachbuilt shell construction, in two-door, two-seater open sports car style. Body skeleton of seasoned ash, with steel body skin panels. Separate front and rear wings and running boards. Exposed spare wheel at rear, fixed to exterior slab-shaped fuel tank. Build-up hood, and perspex (removable side screens and rear quarter window panels. Fold-down windscreen fitted as standard. No factory hard-top option.
Dimensions	Overall length 12ft 3in (374 cm); Overall width 4ft 11.7in (151.8 cm); Overall height 4ft 4.5in (134 cm). Unladen weight (approx) 1,930 lb (877 kg).
Electrical system	12 volt, 51 amp-hr battery mounted on engine side of scuttle/firewall. Positive earth system, with Lucas components.
Fuel system	Fuel tank mounted outside main bodywork, at the tail, with spare wheel clamped to framework behind that. 12 Imperial gallons (54.5 litres). Typical fuel consumption about 25 mpg (11.4 litres/100 km).
Performance	Maximum speed 80 mph. Maximum speeds in gears, 3rd gear 64 mph; 2nd gear 43 mph; 1st gear 26 mph. Acceleration: 0-60mph 19 sec; standing $\frac{1}{4}$-mile 21.5 sec. Fuel consumption 25 mpg average.

TF1500, produced 1954 and 1955

Type	MG TF1500 Sports car
Built	Abingdon, near Oxford
Numbers built	3,400 Basic style, design and layout as for original MG TF, which became retrospectively known as the TF1250, except for the following technical differences:
Engine	BMC/Nuffield Type XPEG. Bore, stroke and capacity 72 x 90 mm, 1466cc (2.83 x 3.54 in, 89.45 cu in); 8.3:1 compression ratio. Maximum power 63 bhp (net) at 5,000 rpm. Maximum torque 76 lb ft at 3,000 rpm.
Performance	Maximum speed 85 mph. Maximum speeds in gears: 3rd gear 64 mph; 2nd gear 43 mph; 1st gear 26 mph. Acceleration: 0-60 mph 16 sec approx; standing $\frac{1}{4}$-mile 20.5 sec approx. 30 mpg average.

TF production breakdown:

Home Market	Export Right Hand Drive	Export Left Hand Drive (not USA)	North America Left Hand Drive	C.O.* Right Hand Drive	CKD** Right Hand Drive	Total
Total						
1242	1544	455	6272	2	85	9600
1953 Calendar Year						
78	118	45	1379	–	–	1620
1954 Calendar Year						
962	927	366	4218	2	45	6520
1955 Calendar Year						
202	499	44	675	–	40	1460
1954 'model year' (Sept. 1953 – 24 July 1954)						
992	987	354	3678	2	–	6013
1955 'model year' (14 August 1954 to April 1955)						
250	557	101	2594	–	85	3587

* Chassis only.
** Provided in knock-down form for assembly abroad.

Note: *This table has been compiled from the extensive TF statistical information held by BL Heritage.*

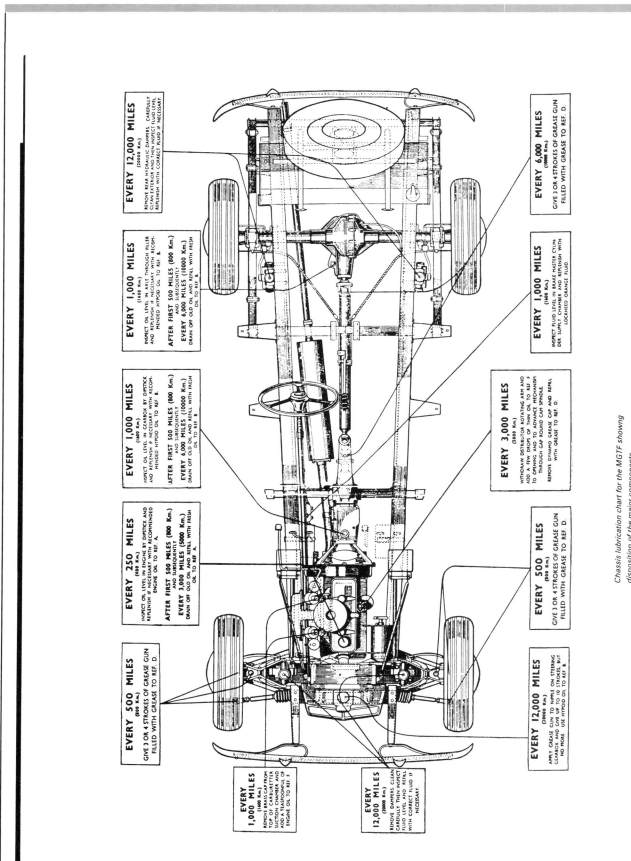

EVERY 12,000 MILES (20000 Km.)
REMOVE REAR HYDRAULIC DAMPERS, CAREFULLY CLEAN EXTERIOR AND THEN INSPECT FLUID LEVEL. REPLENISH WITH CORRECT FLUID IF NECESSARY

EVERY 6,000 MILES (10000 Km.)
GIVE 3 OR 4 STROKES OF GREASE GUN FILLED WITH GREASE TO REF. D.

EVERY 1,000 MILES (1600 Km.)
INSPECT OIL LEVEL IN AXLE THROUGH FILLER AND REPLENISH IF NECESSARY WITH RECOMMENDED HYPOID OIL TO REF. B.
AFTER FIRST 500 MILES (800 Km.) AND SUBSEQUENTLY
EVERY 6,000 MILES (10000 Km.) DRAIN OFF OLD OIL AND REFILL WITH FRESH OIL TO REF. B.

EVERY 1,000 MILES (1600 Km.)
INSPECT FLUID LEVEL IN BRAKE MASTER CYLINDER. SUPPLY CHAMBER AND REPLENISH WITH LOCKHEED ORANGE FLUID

EVERY 1,000 MILES (1600 Km.)
INSPECT OIL LEVEL IN GEARBOX BY DIPSTICK AND REPLENISH IF NECESSARY WITH RECOMMENDED HYPOID OIL TO REF. B.
AFTER FIRST 500 MILES (800 Km.) AND SUBSEQUENTLY
EVERY 6,000 MILES (10000 Km.) DRAIN OFF OLD OIL AND REFILL WITH FRESH OIL TO REF. B.

EVERY 3,000 MILES (5000 Km.)
WITHDRAW DISTRIBUTOR ROTATING ARM AND ADD A FEW DROPS OF THIN OIL TO REF. F TO OPENING AND TO ADVANCE MECHANISM THROUGH GAP ROUND CAM SPINDLE. REMOVE DYNAMO GREASE CAP AND REFILL WITH GREASE TO REF. D.

EVERY 250 MILES (400 Km.)
INSPECT OIL LEVEL IN ENGINE BY DIPSTICK AND REPLENISH IF NECESSARY WITH RECOMMENDED ENGINE OIL TO REF. A.
AFTER FIRST 500 MILES (800 Km.) AND SUBSEQUENTLY
EVERY 3,000 MILES (5000 Km.) DRAIN OFF OLD OIL AND REFILL WITH FRESH OIL TO REF. A.

EVERY 500 MILES (800 Km.)
GIVE 3 OR 4 STROKES OF GREASE GUN FILLED WITH GREASE TO REF. D.

EVERY 500 MILES (800 Km.)
GIVE 3 OR 4 STROKES OF GREASE GUN FILLED WITH GREASE TO REF. D.

EVERY 12,000 MILES (20000 Km.)
APPLY GREASE GUN TO NIPPLE ON STEERING GEARBOX AND GIVE UP TO 10 STROKES, BUT NO MORE. USE HYPOID OIL TO REF. B.

EVERY 1,000 MILES (1600 Km.)
REMOVE BRASS CAP FROM TOP OF CARBURETTER SUCTION CHAMBER AND ADD A TEASPOONFUL OF ENGINE OIL TO REF. F.

EVERY 12,000 MILES (20000 Km.)
REMOVE DAMPERS, CLEAN CAREFULLY THEN INSPECT FLUID LEVEL AND REFILL WITH CORRECT FLUID IF NECESSARY.

Chassis lubrication chart for the MGTF showing disposition of the major components.

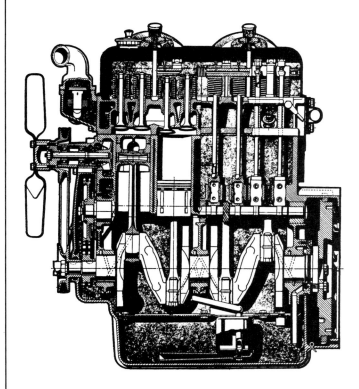

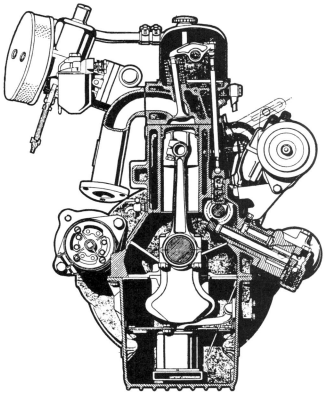

Cross-sectional views of the XPAG and XPEG type engine.

ROAD TEST

MOTOR week ending May 17 1975

Some say that the TF was the last true sports car ever to be built. Certainly for MG it marked the close of a golden era which saw the marque carve its niche in motoring history. Nostalgia is a very personal thing. For Tony Scott, a mere five-year-old in '54, it means the exciting sight and sound of a two seater rag top in the graceful form of an MG TF. Twenty-one years later his chance to drive the model came and here he relates the tale of 5 BMG, a quite remarkable car. Pictures by Peter Burn

By the law of averages 5 BMG should have met its brethren, in that great scrapyard in the sky, ages ago. Those models that remain have either undergone major rebuilds or are a sorry example of a once fine car. Few are genuinely original or as good as they were when new.

But 5 BMG, a graceful creation in deep maroon and bearing the legend MG on its fire-grate radiator grille, is. By a quirk of fate the car (a 1250 MG TF by any dispassionate description) has covered fewer than 18,000 miles since it was driven off the Abingdon production line in 1954.

It was registered at a time when beer cost a few pence a pint, cigarettes around 1s 2d for 10 and Roger Bannister had just stunned the world by becoming the first man to run the mile in under four minutes.

The ending of food rationing in Britain marked the passing austerity of the war years. Life was for living, and driving on our comparatively uncluttered roads was a joy. The summer of '54 was a good one and the only form of real motoring was the rag top variety. For most sporting motorists that meant MG.

The TF wasn't at all quick by today's standards. Around 80 mph was it maximum speed and nowadays any 1300 Escort ought to reach 60 mph in about half the time the TF took. But then if you wanted real speed you bought one of those unbelievably rapid Jaguar XK120s. They'd just been launched.

New the TF cost around £800 in Britain and whatever it lost to bigger, faster saloons of its era, it more than compensated for on sheer agility and fun value. The precision of its rack and pinion steering, an excellent, short shift floor gearchange, fabulous driving position and rorty exhaust bark all combined to make the diminutive MG a desirable piece of machinery.

Moreover the TF looked right; it was the very personification of the term sports car. The model could have almost invented the description "rakish"; everything about it smacked of speed. That long, graceful bonnet and the beautifully sculptured wings blending into the then contemporary running boards. All combined to give the car a certain, undefinable something.

As the owner of something rather dashing you naturally had to live up to the image: the dashing adventurer bit. Once ensconced behind the big rim steering wheel you automatically became something of an heroic pleasure seeker. As Alan Coren says in one of the excellent MG ads, "The sort of bloke with the enviable gift of twitching something volatile out of the wet on a dodgy corner."

And envied you were. £800 was a lot of money in '54. In fact, most of the cars went to our wealthy cousins of the Americas. But not this one. Ordered with its special maroon paint finish the car went to William Barlow, of Haslemere, Surrey, where it stayed, spending a large part of its life on chocks, until its owner's demise in 1971. Passed on to Mr Barlow's son-in-law, the car then found its way into the hands of the people at Old Park Garage, Farnham.

A chap from Yately bought the TF in '71 but never used it. After a further two years on chocks the car was offered to Les Archer of the Les Archer Sports Car Centre, Farnborough. Les, one-time world champion moto-cross bike rider and possessor of more than 200 trophies garnered from the sport, bought the car. He had the bumpers re-chromed, had the wire wheels cleaned and the perspex rear panel in the hood replaced. Otherwise it's quite original. Even the side screens for the hood are still wrapped up in brown paper bearing a May '54 postal date!

We came across the car merely by chance. Les, a regular advertiser of sports cars in Motor had sent in a list of vehicles to be displayed in our pages. The list included the TF which, at the last minute, Les had obviously decided to withdraw as he'd scored it through.

A 'phone call elicited the fact that the car was a genuine one-owner, low mileage model. He withdrew it from our pages simply because a Belgian had walked into his showroom and offered him £3000 in cash. Having recovered from toppling over the bonnets of some assorted Triumphs and MGs Les mustered the courage to say "no." Even when the Belgian increased his offer to gold bar (which would appreciate rather than devalue in the form of pounds) Les held his ground. The Belgian went away a disappointed man.

Which is how we got to drive the car. The assignation was viewed with relish, especially as we had one of the new Federal spec 1500 MG Midgets on test at the time. The entire plan was to compare the two. However, since the Federal car will be compared directly with its like-engined counterpart, the 1500 Spitfire, in next week's issue there's no point in revealing all. Suffice to say that the new car is very much quicker than the old but possesses nothing like the same charm.

The January test date dawned reasonably fine. Photographer Peter Burn and I were to rendez-vous at Les Archer's establishment at nine, and circulate around the Farnborough district for pictures and driving impressions. Most of the time was spent amid the scenic splendour of Frencham Ponds.

First impressions are always the most vivid so here they are, directly as spoke into the mouthpiece of the office tape-recording machine: doors open outwards from rear hinges (strange!); smell of natural leather pervading the interior; seats very comfortable with lots of lateral support but no belts (how vulnerable I feel!). Pulling the starter motor button brings the engine into rorty life. At idle it ticks over like a sewing machine but the rev counter flickers wildly. Gauges include a speedo with integral timepiece, water, amp and oil gauges, plus a rev counter which reads to 6500 without a red line. Shall use four and bit rather than risk a demolition exercise. Engine doesn't seem to have an awful lot of urge. Gearchange is nice but second seems rather high. Best changes are the slow ones. Clutch a bit sharp. Brake travel is excessive but they're there if you tread on them hard. Handbrake is the fly-off sort. Exhaust bark is fantastic: a real ego booster! Ride extremely firm, so much so that biggish bumps lift you bodily from the seat while the steering, which is very direct, tends to writhe in an endeavour to break free of your grasp. Castor action is lovely. Cockpit is rather cramped; my legs have disappeared down the long, narrow footwell. Pedals very close. Without the side screens on there's an incredible draught through the side. With the hood down the wind tends to billow over the shallow screen tossing my hair into a tangled mess. The car oversteers just like the current Midget but is easily caught. Verdict: a safe yet entertaining car.

All this happened in January. Les still has the car and I'm more than ever convinced that I should buy an old MG. The TF I love but could never afford. Now, if anybody knows of a P-type Midget in reasonable shape that's looking for a good home. . . .

The MG TF 1250 in full flight. The lines are classic while the car's condition is almost beyond belief. Les Archer has been offered three grand for the car but wants to pair it with an R-R Shadow he's got at £14,000 the two

Operations centre (top) plus the heart of things (below). In '54 plastic interiors were the option rather than the natural thing as was the case with the TF. Spot the grime (below); 21 years haven't left a mark

DRIVING IMPRESSIONS

MG TF Driving Impressions

Because of the scarcity of historical road test material on the MG TF the opportunity was taken to carry out a road test specially for this Super Profile.

Firstly I must make it clear that this is not intended to be a road test in the conventional sense, rather it is intended to portray to the reader the 'feel' of the MG TF from the point of view of somebody who has never before had the opportunity of driving this particular model. It is also intended to reflect how the TF fares in modern driving conditions and stands up in relation to the qualities of modern cars which we all take for granted, but which are, in fact, the result of continuous development.

John Haynes kindly provided a 1250cc, 1955 MG TF and put no restrictions upon what could be done with the car. Aware that, even on its launch, the TF was something of an anachronism we wanted to make a brief comparison with a contemporary sports car which would have fallen in approximately the same purchase price bracket — the Triumph TR2 would have been the obvious choice but, unfortunately, none was available. The closest we could get

was a TR3 of 1962 vintage, also from John Haynes' collection. Obviously this was something of a compromise, but as the TR3 is not far removed from the TR2 in terms of its specification it was felt that the comparison was valid within the spirit of this test — you may feel otherwise ...

SCV 730, the TF tested, has been fully restored, including a fully rebuilt engine not yet fully run in, and has been used since the restoration was completed giving it a comfortable feel instead of the forbidding untouchability of a *concours d'elegance* winner. In fact it's probably fair to say that it represents how a very young TF would have appeared and felt in the fifties. However, although this particular car is in good mechanical health it is only fair to point out that it is not necessarily typical of the model and may have superior or inferior performance in some areas.

The test took place in Somerset on a glorious Summer's day with the sun shining from a cloudless sky and the temperature hovering around eighty degrees. As I approached the TF, its brilliant scarlet paint shimmering and its chrome sparkling, I could not help but reflect upon what a pretty car it is — an unusual adjective to describe a car, I know, but the TF's harmony and almost contrived 'classic British sports car' appearance do make it look as though it was designed to be part of the set for a chocolate box photograph.

From my vantage point, at over six feet, the car appears to be remarkably low; an impression reinforced when I had to bend almost double to release the door catch on the forward opening door. And how to get in? The grey leather driver's bucket seat, already as far back as it will go, nevertheless has its squab part-way under the large, and very vertical, steering wheel and the footwell seems to stretch away into infinity ... In the end two methods achieved the desired end. Either one could stand with one's back to the door, insert the left leg, place the left hand on the seat and then sort of flop into the seat pulling in the other leg afterwards or, and marginally easier, lower oneself into the seat sideways, swivel round and in so doing drag the knees beneath the wheel and then push the legs down into the footwell — neither very elegant and I would have thought almost impossible with the hood up. I suspect too, that even those of average height would find entry an awkward manoeuvre — and this feature of the TF must have cramped the style of the dashing young men of the fifties who were out to impress the girls!

Still, I'm now installed in the pilot's seat and immediately know that this is no modern car. For a start I seem to be sitting bolt upright and the steering wheel is almost thrust against my chest even though the foot pedals are at a comfortable distance for outstretched legs. Gone are the

1. The TF in its element; a fast country road in the summer sunshine.

familiar flat rocker switches and almost plastic dashpanel of the modern car together with its padded and relatively small steering wheel. Instead, I'm faced by a wildly curved dashpanel whose focal point is a group of three matching instruments complete with chrome bezels: from left to right they are the speedometer with increments up to 105mph and incorporating mileometer, trip meter and clock; in the centre a combination instrument comprising water temperature, oil pressure to 100psi and ammeter; then, the last major gauge, the tachometer, is obscured by the steering wheel. The tachometer reads to 6500rpm but carries no red line. Dotted around these instruments are various matching black control knobs and switches and the chrome bezel of the ignition switch. On each side of the instrument panel is an open cubby hole and at the extreme right hand end of the dashboard is a single trafficator switch parked in the central position. Across the top of the dashboard, and looking somewhat like eyebrows, is a well padded crash roll — not a lot of use to the driver whose ribs would have been well and truly cracked by the protruding boss of the standard steel-spoked steering wheel long before his unrestrained body got anywhere near the crash roll! Mounted centrally on the top of the dashboard is a chrome-framed rear view mirror.

What I should have said by now, of course, is that octagons abound within the car — every instrument is octagonal as is the bezel and central decoration of each, every knob is octagonal, there

is an octagon in the gearlever knob and even the steering boss carries an octagonal motif — I get the impression that the designer probably had to forcibly restrained to prevent his adorning the car with an octagonal steering wheel ...

The view over the bonnet, framed by the windscreen surround, is wonderful. One's eye is first taken by the humps in the scuttle directly before both driver and passenger, which seem to beg the fitting of aero screens and the donning of a leather flying cap and goggles. Then the eye is carried forward, along the line of the central bonnet hinge to the, would you believe, octagonal radiator cap which is flanked by the almost sensuously curved headlamp nacelles and front wings. All of which for me at least heightens the feeling that this was a car created to reflect the public's image of what a sports car should look like, rather than what a sports car should do. If you like, an inversion of the old maxim that 'form follows function'.

The key is already in the ignition so, after jiggling the gearlever, which immediately beneath the instrument panel is well placed for me, to ensure that

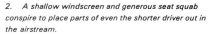

2. A shallow windscreen and generous seat squab conspire to place parts of even the shorter driver out in the airstream.

it's in neutral, I turn the ignition key and pull the starter knob behind the steering wheel — the engine immediately bursts into life and settles down to a steady tickover although with some hunting as if the mixture is slightly too rich. (No choke was necessary as the car had been thoroughly warmed up before my arrival). The ohv engine sounds completely modern, with none of the flat note of the sidevalves which abounded in its day. On blipping the throttle engine response seems slow: probably the inertia of a relatively heavy flywheel and characteristic of long stroke engines.

I press the clutch, push the gearlever over to the left and forwards and although slightly stiff it engages first gear very positively and with no 'clunk'. After pulling up briefly on the fly-off handbrake, and lowering it to the floor I let up the clutch and I'm on my way with no drama at all.

For the first few miles I take it easy getting used to the car, and just enjoying open air motoring on one of those days when it's the *only*

3. *The last of a vintage tradition about to be overhauled easily by a precocious contemporary.*

way to travel. I had one problem as soon as I was under way — the windscreen rail was exactly at eye level, so I had to wriggle down into the seat so that I could peer just beneath it!

The clutch was of medium weight and travel and completely smooth in its operation, whilst the gearchange was a little stiff but in a very positive gate — there being no discernible detent to prevent the accidental engagement of reverse. Some deliberation was definitely needed when changing gear, particularly down through the box. I found the best technique was to press the clutch and bring the gearlever into neutral, count one, two, and then move the gearlever down into the next gear before releasing the clutch pedal again. There was no advantage in double de-clutching that I could discern.

When new the smaller engine TF's most natural cruising speed is about 45-50 mph. At this speed the car had very neutral handling and would proceed uphill and down dale with very little loss, or gain, in performance. It quickly became obvious that there was little benefit to be had from stirring the gearbox: the car had a very narrow optimum rev band determined by engine inertia at the lower end and breathlessness at the higher end. Within its natural rev band the engine provides impressive torque for a 1250cc unit even if it is rather dictatorial in terms of how you can drive the car. At all speeds, on the open road, the exhaust note is strident and sounds more sporty than the engine which produces it really is: still it is a pleasant accompaniment to driving the TF, although I imagine it could become wearing on a longer journey.

The car's ride was firm, but not harsh. The impression I got was that in fact the suspension was stiff but there was so much compliance in the chassis that this stiffness was not generally felt by the occupants of the car. I should add that this particular TF was shod with modern radial tyres: something its suspension was never designed to cope with.

Performance-wise it has to be said that the 1250 TF is not particularly fast; a situation that was much improved with the introduction of the 1500 model and finally resolved by the MGA which was a geniune 100 mph sports car.

As I have said before, up to an indicated 50mph the handling of this car was neutral and not at all quirky but, pressed beyond this speed, things changed dramatically. At just over 50mph the scuttle would begin to quake and a disturbing front wheel shimmy would set in — although this never developed to dangerous proportions and was driven through by the time 55mph was indicated. Scuttle and front wing shaking persisted right up to the highest speed I obtained in the car, an indicated 68mph on a long stretch of dual carriageway. (It was pointed out after the test that the car had been standing during the winter months and may well have developed flat spots in the tyres.) winter months and may well have developed flat spots in the tyres.)

The TF's brakes were always reassuringly powerful with no sign of bias but did need relatively heavy pedal pressure and lacked any feel. The steering too, was reassuring and precise, although front end hopping could change the car's line in a bumpy corner, even at fairly slow speeds. Despite the size of the steering wheel, the steering was stiffish until around 20mph was reached. Of course this stiffness may well have been due to the radial tyres.

My most unpleasant moment with the TF came at the apex of a sweeping but bumpy country bend taken at about 50mph. Normally, the TF displayed typical rear-wheel-drive understeer during faster cornering with no propensity

towards lurching or sudden changes of attitude. However, on this particular left-hand bend the surface bumps set the front end of the car pogoing across the road towards the outside of the bend: in fact the front end of the car moved a good six feet off the cornering line and well over the centre of the road …

I enjoyed my time with the TF and many of the criticisms I have levelled would only be valid if directed at a sports car. In my opinion the TF is not, and never has been, a sports car. What it is, is a wonderful touring car – not a grand tourer: it doesn't have the weather protection or luggage accommodation – that is enormous fun on a fine day when the driver is not in a rush. And the TF will always be a beautiful car to look at …

I have avoided comparison with the Triumph TR3 until this point, because as sports cars there is no comparison: the TR feels as if it is from a different era, although its birth is contemporary with the launch of the TF.

TYS 896 is also finished in brilliant red and has been well used since its restoration. There the similarity ends for, although the TR, too, feels very dated in some respects, it is a sports car from the ground up and cries out to be driven hard and fast – conspiring with the driver in these demands.

Although the TR has the advantage of a bigger engine, it is not the capacity which makes the difference but rather the engine's character. This unit has a wide usable rev range, but still retains bags of torque: features which, allied with a positive and quick gearchange and well chosen ratios, make the car very responsive indeed. The TR also has quicker

steering than the TF and more sensitive brakes. Altogether, it's a package which rewards the hard-working driver with great driving pleasure and always leaves him or her with the feeling of wanting to get back behind the wheel as soon as possible. It would probably be completely exhausting as a tourer!

G. B. Wake

OWNER'S VIEW

Anyone who owns an MG TF in the 1980s tends to use it sparingly, for pleasure (and nostalgia?) only, but still enjoys it as a real open-topped sports car, as these short interviews confirm.

The first talk was with Bernard Jesty, who also provided the beautifully preserved cream TF1250 for us to photograph, to illustrate these pages:

JE: Tell me when you bought this car, and why?
BJ: I actually found this one in 1979, and I bought it just because I like T-Types. But it wasn't my first MG ...
JE: Tell me more?
BJ: In fact, the first MG I ever owned was a TC registered MAF 92, which I bought in Cornwall and used for about 18 months. When I was a younger man I never had an MG because I could never afford one! Then I saw this TF, bought it, decided my TC wasn't up to the same standard, stripped it out, and rebuilt it! Then I bought another TC as a complete and utter wreck, and rebuilt that one as well, side by side!
The advantage with all T-Types, of course, is that you can take everything apart — wings, doors and bonnet, they can all be un-bolted.

JE: Why did you buy this one, particularly?
BJ: Oh, it was a coincidence, really — I happened to go past a garage near Yeovil, where it was for sale!
JE: Was it in good condition then?
BJ: Yes, absolutely as you see it. I've had virtually nothing to do to it, and the body shell is good, so it must have been restored at one time.
JE: Have you needed to buy parts at all, and was it difficult?
BJ: Very few, at all, but the spares position is very good, mechanically and bodily. I think you could buy everything for a TF, if you wanted it.
JE: Do you use it much, and regularly?
BJ: Not really. In fact in four years I've only done about 2,200 miles — but I enjoy all of them!
JE: Do you enter it in any sporting events, or concours?
BJ: No, not this one, though it's a good car. I concentrated on my TC for that sort of thing, very successfully. But the concours standard is extremely high nowadays.
JE: You told me earlier that you had four T-Series cars, but sold three of them and kept this TF. Why?
BJ: This one feels better on the road than the TCs — the other three MGs of mine were all TCs — it's got rack and pinion steering, which is very accurate, and independent front suspension, which makes it much softer. It has a much better ride than the TCs.
JE: What else do you like about the car?
BJ: I like the looks of course, especially from the driving seat, through the windscreen and along the bonnet. Inside, of course, it's a bit more civilised, and all the controls work nicely. Mechanically, it is simple enough, so that I will be able to tackle all the mechanical work when the time comes. I don't intend to sell it, so there may be work to do, one day ...
JE: Are you in any of the one-make MG clubs?

BJ: Yes, the MG Owner's Club. They offer very valuable services, technical advice, and reprinted material. You can get most of the practical information you'll ever need from them.
JE: What will happen if ever it does start to give trouble?
BJ: As I said, I should be able to tackle mechanical work, but not bodies, no. I would have to consult a specialist for that. Like most people, I don't have the right sort of equipment to rebuild the body. Incidentally, although the body shell can be stripped down, it isn't always a one-man job — you can loosen off the bonnet, by unscrewing the centre bar, but it is an awkward, two-man job, to lift it clear.
JE: Are you still as happy with it now, as you were when you bought it five years ago?
BJ: Oh yes, for driving round with the top down, in fine sunny weather, there's nothing better. It's not as much fun in the wet, though. It's a small, compact, little sports car, too, which helps.

Some MG TF owners, however, not only use their cars much more regularly, but have also tackled major rebuilds to get them to 'better-than-new' condition. One of them is a Midlands enthusiast, Tony Stafford:

JE: Are you an MG owner from way back?
TS: Yes, for 25 years now. All my life I've been involved with cars, having been an apprentice in a local garage, then working on them in the Air Force, then I worked in the motor industry in the Midlands.
JE: So, where did it all start?
TS: The first MG I bought was a TD, which I had for about two years. I regretted selling it two minutes after it had gone! Then I bought myself an MGA, a nice little car but I hadn't got the same feeling for it. I always promised myself a TF when the right one came along ...
JE: And then?
TS: I found my car in a garage in

Wakefield, more than 10 years ago, buried under a pile of dumped bits. It was really scrap, for the back axle was locked solid – I only paid £1,250 for it.

JE: Did you tackle your own rebuild?

TS: Oh yes, I did everything – body off the chassis, the lot. It wasn't as easy to rebuild a TF then, as now, for the parts situation was difficult. For instance, you couldn't buy a set of doors – I had to make the ash frames for the doors, *and* skin them myself! Luckily, after a rebore, all the muck and rust in the engine was cleared out, and with a reground crank it was fine. The axle too, was stripped, given new bearings and so on, and works well. Even the gearbox had a broken layshaft when I bought it! It took about 18 months of my spare time – actually *all* my spare time.

JE: Did it need new body framing?

TS: Yes, about 50 per cent of the wood, mostly the lower parts.

JE: Did anything beat you?

TS: Yes, just the seats. I borrowed my wife's sewing machine, but there was no way it could cope with Connolly leather facings, so I had to pay for the seats to be retrimmed. But nothing else – even my paint spraying kit cost less than £100!

JE: How much have you used the car over the years?

TS: In 1983 I had a 3,000 + mile trip to West Germany, Luxembourg and Belgium, and about 6,500 miles during the year. I use it a lot. Incidentally the speedometer reads 84,000 miles, and that's the second time round!

JE: Does this usage mean that you worry about wearing it out?

TS: No, not at all. If anything wears out, I replace it. You can get anything for a TF these days. I service the car every 2,000 miles anyway, though I think the manual recommends 3,000 miles. Cleaning, waxing, and polishing is done pretty often, and if I have had it out in the rain, even if I get home after midnight, I garage it, then get the leather out to wipe it all down. That doesn't take long – only about an hour.

JE: Do you enter it in motor sport, or concours contests?

TS: Not in competitions, but I often show it, yes. The standard for TFs is very high, and mine is reputedly the best in the MG Owners' Club, probably one of the best in the UK. But the standards are now so high that some concours owners don't use their cars, just show them, whereas I like to drive mine as well.

JE: Why do you like the TF so much – compared, say, with the MGA?

TS: I think it is the prettiest sports car MG ever made. People admire them, and now of course they are quite rare in this country. I've had other MGs, Jaguars and things, but I love driving the TF. You can drive it all day at 55/60 mph, but perhaps not use it on motorways and thrash it all that much – it gets noisy and blowy with the hood down.

JE: Any problems with your TF?

TS: It has never let me down, except that I broke the gearbox once, chipping teeth off second gear. The TF's box is known to have a weaker lay gear, say, than the TC, which was very strong. The other problems I do have, by the way, are that the pedals are close together, rather like the Morris Minor, and you tend to wonder where you can put your left foot.

JE: Are you a member of a major MG club?

TS: Yes, I'm in the MG Owner's Club, and the Octagon Club. I'm not in the MG Car Club as well, not just because they mainly concentrate on motor sport, but because I just don't have time to be involved and go to meetings of so many clubs.

The MG Owners' Club helps a lot, with technical contacts, but the Octogan Club is a very nice, small, organisation.

JE: Lastly, I wouldn't insult you by asking what your car is worth, but has the notional value of TFs now gone silly?

TS: A very difficult question to answer. They say that a concours example of a TF was worth more than £10,000 in 1983, and I certainly saw a car advertised for £7,500 in the same year which *I* thought was ripe for a rebuild! About six to seven years ago, I guess if you wanted to sell a TF, it had to be to the USA, but now a TF is not fetching any more there than it is in the UK. But that explains why they are now so rare in this country.

BUYING

Because the MG TF has always had such a high reputation in the 'classic' or 'collector's' market place, I suppose it is inevitable that the present-day supply is somewhat limited, especially in the UK where the cars were originally manufactured. To remind you — of the 9,600 TFs made between 1953 and 1955, only 1,242 were delivered to British customers, and no fewer than 6,272 went to the USA at first. In recent years I know that a good few of the UK's surviving TFs have been exported to the USA, which by now must hold most of the surviving cars.

In general, there is no reason for loving one type of TF, and hating the other, though I think it is generally agreed that the TF1500 was a better, more lusty, derivative than the original, and that the cars are prettier when fitted with centre-lock wire spoke wheels.

When the MG TF dropped out of production in 1955, its retail price was £780 (total) in the UK, and $1,995 in the USA, but values dropped considerably in the next few years as the sleek, modern, MGA won the hearts of MG enthusiasts all over the world. By the mid-1960s a TF was 'going for a song' virtually anywhere, and it was only at the beginning of the 1970s that values began to climb again. In 1973, when Britain's first 'classic' magazine, *Thoroughbred & Classic cars,* was founded, you could buy a scruffy, but roadworthy, TF for £700, and something approaching a 'concours' example for less than £2,000. Naturally it isn't wise to quote 'current' values in a book which is going to be on sale for some time, but in the early 1980s, after the second oil price scare had come and gone, a good-condition UK TF would fetch more than £6,000, and a similar-grade car in the USA up to $10,000. For truly 'concours' examples you could double that! No wonder that Naylors, the UK restoration specialists, thought it worth marketing a replica, with modern BL power train, for £12,000 in 1984!

Because the TF was built with a wooden body skeleton, because it was built in considerable numbers, and because it was built down to a price, it tended to start wearing out and rotting away quite early in its life. Even though it was an MG! Quite a high proportion of all the TFs built will now have gone on to that great parking lot in the sky, and those which survive will have been restored at least once, or be in a pretty desperate state by now. That can apply both to the body shells, which were pretty vulnerable to rot, and to the chassis/mechanical line-up as well.

Even though you can find spare parts for just about every feature on the cars, these tend to be expensive these days (especially body panels), so anyone looking to buy a TF should be sure to look carefully. For convenience, I have split my advice into two sections:

Body shell and wood

Originally, of course, this was built by the Morris Bodies branch in Coventry, merely being finished off and mated with the rest of the car at Abingdon. The main structure was in ash, which even after correct seasoning could never be stopped from rotting through, while the body panels were all in sheet steel. It is possible, though not likely, that a restored car may have had light alloy panels fitted instead of steel, which is a help — but then such a car would no longer be original, and that makes it less valuable...

Wherever moisture can get at the wood, it will eventually rot it. Since most of the wood is covered up by steel panelling, or by trim, you may never know that rot is well advanced, until it is too late. Look for evidence wherever you can see the wood, or remove trim panels to check further. The bottom of doors, the door pillars, the plywood areas around the tail, and the wheel-arch regions are all possible 'horror' points.

Sagging door hinges tell their own story (it doesn't help to know that TCs were worse!), and the woodwork at the front of the door aperture (where the door has repeatedly been slammed on to it) may have wilted after years of abuse. The T-Series MGs are like Morgans — likely to rot badly from new, but usually much better after a careful rebuild, when there has been more time for pre-assembly protection of the wood, before the steel cladding is added. For that reason, I would always suggest that a *properly* restored TF is a better long-term bet than one of those 'absolutely original, Old Boy' cars you hear about. New woodwork is available, either in sections, or as a complete skeleton, but not from the factory — there is nothing at all available from MG after all these years. Specialists, like Naylors in the UK and their equivalent overseas, provide an excellent service.

You can also find a lot of rust — everywhere from frilly wings (expensive to replace because of their size and shape) to inner rear wheel arches, bulkheads to lower door skins, petrol tanks (near the fixings) to any fixing hole (for instance, wing mirrors, side lamps, windscreens, and so on). That is the bad news — the good news is that most of the extremities of a TF body – wings, engine bay sides, doors, rear wings, petrol tank, for instance – are easily unbolted from their neighbour. One TF owner I talked to described his car as 'grown-up construction kit' building, and I knew what he meant...

Most soft trim items and carpets have been remanufactured these days, and it is always nice to see a TF with the tonneau cover which helps to keep the rain out, the aero-screens fitted behind the folding windscreen, and a proper hood in a material known as 'Double Duck'. Beware – some replacement hoods were not supplied in this material, but rather nastier substitutes – it would be a pity if the one you were considering buying was so afflicted.

Chassis and suspension

Surprisingly enough, the all-box-section TF frame is vulnerable to corrosion, sometimes from the inside, outwards, and the rust usually starts at the rear end first. Where the frame is most heavily stressed – front and rear suspension pick-up points, and the outriggers at each side – is where the cracking inevitably caused will have allowed rust to start and spread. Restoration is of course possible if the corrosion is not too firmly established, but *at a price* you can get complete new sections for a rebuild. Please be sure to check, too, that the frame is not twisted, and that the car has not been crashed, and make sure that places where vital parts (like pedals!) 'hang on' are still in good shape.

At the rear end you only need to check that the leaf springs are in good order, and don't have broken leaves, and that the lever-arm dampers still damp, and don't leak (these can be rebuilt, or new ones purchased, of course). A lack of regular lubrication over the years

may not have helped the spring shackles and pivots to survive, unworn, either.

At the front, check on the lever-arm dampers (the same advice as for the rear), on the feel, tightness, and general condition of the rack and pinion steering and related ball joints, and more particularly on the condition of the upper and lower king post trunnions. Badly worn trunnions will make a noise when the car is manoeuvred at low speeds, the steering will be heavy, the cambers all wrong, and tyre wear uneven. Modern replacements tend to be steel, but they still need regular maintenance. Has the previous owner, or owners, done what the handbook recommends? Especially on TFs which have been rallied, raced, or used in other competitions, check on the hubs – for wear, and for free movements. Hubs and bearings may need attention, and even a short drive, and a ramp inspection, will tell you about their state.

If the brake hydraulics are in good condition (look for leak marks, and for the 'feel' and 'length' of the pedal, not forgetting the action of the fly-off handbrake) there should be little to fear, though juddery braking may mean that the drums themselves have become distorted with excessively hard use. The TF, though, was neither ultra-fast, nor heavy, so the brakes didn't have a very hard time...

Engine and transmission

Everyone loves the XPAG (1,250cc) and XPEG (1,466cc) engines, which are so easy to power-tune and so simple to keep in tune. They seem to love to be revved, and they thrive on hard work, but of course they can, and do, wear out. Don't forget that the youngest of all TF engines, if original, was nearly 30 years old when these words were written. Would *you* have retained an acceptable (50 psi) oil pressure over all those years?

Look for all the obvious signs of wear – noisy tappets, rumbles, heavy oil consumption, blue smoke from the exhaust, and sluggish consumption – and be deeply suspicious of any tendency to use (or lose) water. Personally I wouldn't want to buy a TF with an extensively modified engine, as this is automatically going to put higher loads on tappets, valve gear, pistons and bearing shells. A good standard tune is really a much more satisfactory proposition. I don't know of any major differences in behaviour between the XPAG and XPEG types.

Be sure, incidentally, that the carburettors are correctly balanced and tuned, for this can make so much difference to general response, performance and fuel economy.

The weakness in the transmission is not only at the rear axle, where there may already have been (or, one day, will be) trouble with the ring and pinion set, but in the gearbox itself, which is not nearly strong enough for this job – it was, after all, conceived in the 1930s for the humble Morris 10 application! Expect every TF, one day, to suffer from wear to the layshaft, the gears themselves and the bearings. The clutch, at least, should not often 'come out in sympathy'.

Perhaps these are harsh words for the transmission, whose feel should be slick, and whose changes should be sweet, but it is a fact that the box (and the TF, in relation to the rest of the T-Series) was near the end of its life.

In summary, you should always remember that the MG TF was a quantity-produced motor car, built around mass-production components, sometimes tuned nearly to the limits of their potential, and that you should not, therefore, expect to find miracles. Further, although nearly every item on the car can be replaced, rebuilt, or competently repaired, it may not be a cheap operation.

Best Buys? I wouldn't have much hesitation in recommending a TF1500, complete with wire spoke wheels, preferably a car which has either lived in a dry climate for most of its life, or one which has been thoroughly and competently restored, around a new and rot-proofed wooden

skeleton. That sort of TF, if lovingly owned, should be ready to give further decades of service and pleasure.

CLUBS, SPECIALISTS & BOOKS

Clubs

Although there is no specialist club catering specifically for the MG TF, several large, long-established, and important clubs look after the needs of all MG owners.

In the UK, these are:

MG Owners' Club,
2/4 Station Road,
Swavesey,
Cambridge.
Tel: 0954-31125

This is the largest one-make club in the country, and has a large, well-organised, system of keeping members in touch with parts suppliers, and restoration specialists.

MG Car Club,
67 Wide Bargate,
Boston,
Lincolnshire.
Tel: 0205-64301

This club concentrates on fellowship, and motor sport, rather than on restoration, promoting trials, race meetings, as well as providing technical advice and spares assistance. There are branches of the MG Car Club all round the world, this club being particularly strong in the USA. There is also a thriving T Register in the USA.

Octagon Car Club,
Rapier Retreat,
Weston-under-Lizard,
Shifnal,
Shropshire.
Tel: 021-558-1431
Ext 374

This club is particularly interested in T-Series MGs.

Specialists

As this book will be read in many countries, there is no point only in quoting specialists in the UK. It is enough to say that there is expertise available all around the world, particularly in the UK, and in the USA. The clubs will happily put members in touch with specialist suppliers of parts, literature, or restoration advice. It is possible to have complete body reconstruction, and the major rebuilding of any part of the engine, transmission, and running gear.

Books

There is no other book specifically about the MG TF, but there are several existing publications about MGs, and T-Series cars in particular, which provide further reading. Among them are:

The Immortal T-Series, by Chris Harvey.
A big, lavishly illustrated volume, with many colour pictures, covering all T-Series cars built, from 1936 to 1955. Published by Oxford Illustrated Press.

The T-Series MGs, a Collector's Guide, by Graham Robson.
A completely factual volume about the entire T-Series range, including production figures, and many other statistics – by the author of this Superprofile. Published by Motor Racing Publications.

The T-Series Handbook, by Dick Knudson and F.E. Old III.

Published in North America, this concentrates on the nuts-and-bolts history of the cars built after 1945, and includes much service and maintenance information. As detailed as anything published in the UK. Published by the New England T Register Ltd.

MG TF, 1953-1955, by Brooklands Books.
Like other BBs, this is compiled as reprints of original material, from all around the world, of magazine tests and impressions of the TF. Softback, but good value. Published by Brooklands Books.

More general reading is provided by:
MG by McComb, by Wilson McComb.
The acknowledged 'standard work' on the entire history of the MG marque, by a writer who knew many MG personalities well. Published by Osprey.

MG 1911 to 1978, by Peter Filby.
One of the well-known Haynes 'Mini-Marque' series, encapsulating the entire story to 1978, and naturally including the T-Series. Published by Haynes.

Tuning and Maintenance of MG Cars, by Philip H. Smith.
This book covers the T-series engines, including the XPAG, in detail. Published by Haynes.

Many other MG titles have been published, covering other model ranges, and several reprints of Workshop Manuals (including T-Series models) are also available.

One other excellent book, long out of print, covers the mechanical and tuning aspects of earlier MGs and T-Series cars including the TF. This is the splendid work by John Thornley himself:

Maintaining the Breed, by John Thornley.
This can often be found at autojumbles (swapmeets), and in secondhand book shops. Well worth a search.

PHOTO
GALLERY

1

2

1. The T-Series MG family went on sale in 1936, with tuned-Morris parts, and traditional MG-style looks. The TB of 1939 – of which this is a prototype – looked identical, but had the XPAG engine.

2. You could not really pick a TA, from a TB, from a TC by the styling, for there were no give-away badges. The spindly wire wheels, the exposed spare and the slab tank were all typical of the breed though.

3. The TF's direct ancestor was the TD, launched in 1950, which had a new box-section chassis with independent front suspension and the famous 1,250cc XPAG engine.

4. The TD's coil spring independent front suspension was also to be used on the TF, and the MGA which replaced the TF in 1955. The lever-arm dampers also formed the suspension's 'top' wishbone.

5. Some modified T-Series MGs had two sets of lever-arm dampers, like this car. The André units were mounted on the lower wishbones themselves and the links led to the top of the pressed crossmember.

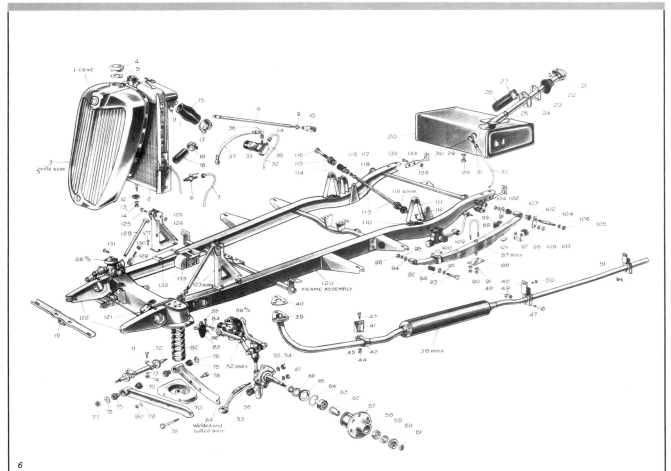

6

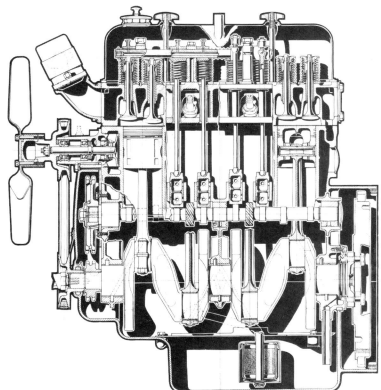

7

6. This, in fact, is the chassis of the MG Y-Series saloon, underslung at the rear, but the general layout was the same as that of the TF sports car and many suspension components were identical. This design dated from 1947.

7. A cross-section view of the Nuffield-designed XPAG engine, as fitted to the TF. It was originally designed by Morris Engines Branch in Coventry, as the XPJM unit, for the Morris 10 of 1938.

8. Strong, simple, and amazingly tuneable – the XPAG engine of 1,250cc, allied to the nice, but none-too-strong, transmission. All TFs had carburettor air cleaners of this type as standard.

9. The TF's engine had its engine oil pump housing outside the sump, with the filter horizontally mounted behind it.

10. The rear of the T-Series chassis – actually this is a TD, but there were no significant changes over the years – showing the location of the springs, dampers, and exhaust pipe run.

11. The T-Series chassis used from 1950 to 1955, for the TD and TF, had box section side members and a stiffening hoop around the passenger footwells.

12. Cecil Kimber, killed some years previously, would have approved of all these octagons, I'm sure! The facia of the TF was entirely different from, and much more stylised than that of the TD which it replaced. For left-hand-drive cars, only the rev-counter and speedometer changed positions in the instrument display.

13. Head-on view of the TF, as pictured in the Nuffield studios in 1953 before production started. Strangely enough, this one has Dunlop racing tyres fitted.

12

13

14   15

16

14. An early-production TF in the studio, showing off the optional luggage grid. Note that this is a left-hand-drive car, which mirrored BMC's hope for massive export sales.

15. The characteristic three-quarter front view of the TF, as it was originally built in 1953. On this car, the centre-lock spoke wheels, and the luggage grid were optional extras.

16. The 'basic' TF was built like this, with perforated disc wheels. The car's centre section was still pure TD, but there was a new nose, and a new more swept tail, rear wings and fuel tank. All-round visibility was surprisingly good with the hood erect.

17. One proposal for replacing the TF came from Nuffield's chief designer, Gerald Palmer, keeping to the long-established chassis, but only this mockup was ever produced.

17

18. The 'TF replacement' by Gerald Palmer might have had this type of facia, with modified TF instruments ahead of the driver's eyes.

19. Under this sleek skin is a much-modified T-Series chassis! The car was raced at Le Mans in 1951 by George Phillips, the styling being by Syd Enever at Abingdon. By 1952 it had evolved...

20. ...into the EX175 prototype, with a new chassis frame to match the style, but still with the TD/TF type of engine and transmission. Eventually it grew up to become the MGA, which replaced the TF in 1955.

18

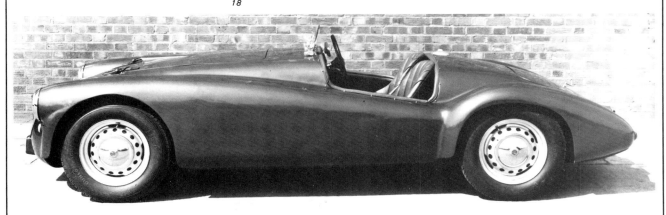

19

20

21

22

23

24

25

22. If you find a real MG TF, as opposed to a replica, the chassis plate will look like this. The chassis number is 1984 – how appropriate, for the picture was also taken in that year! Note the legendary telephone number – Abingdon 251. For years the number was often the first in a model's chassis series (but not the TF, which started from 501).

23. As you can see, the body number was not the same as the chassis number, for on this car the chassis number is 1984. Bodies were constructed at the Morris Bodies Branch in Coventry, then transported to Abingdon by road.

24. The optional Dunlop centre-lock wire spoke wheels exposing the TF's drum brakes. This is a 1984 picture, which excuses the use of 'non-original' radial ply tyres!

25. The spare wheel mounting position, against the slab fuel tank, and with the registration plate above the bumper, its light on top of the plate.

21. The real BMC replacement for the TF Midget was the original Austin-Healey Sprite of 1958, with only a 948cc A-Series engine, and not quite as much performance. This eventually became the next Midget, announced in 1961.

26

27

26. Rear end, rear suspension detail, with the rear spring exposed by the flare of the rear wing. The chrome bumper protects the wings up to a point, but would not withstand a purposeful 'parking' blow. The electrical wiring to the stop/tail/direction indicator lamp is exposed to the build up of road filth.

27. On the TF there is even an MG octagon at the top of the sump dipstick! It is obvious from this close-up shot that the under-bonnet area is well-filled on the near side, with dynamo, distributor and rev-counter drive all in shot.

28. A worm's-eye view of a 30-year-old, but nicely preserved, TF, showing the chassis side members tapering out from the front suspension cross-member, the position of the twin horns, tucked away close to the lower wishbone pivots, and the rather exposed exhaust pipe run.

29. The same worm, having moved a few feet towards the rear, would see the exhaust pipe of the TF running under the line of the rear axle, the smooth sweep of the handbrake cables to each rear brake, and the exposed electrical wiring. The TF was nothing if not simple.

30. By the 1950s, a windscreen that could be folded flat was a rare feature on new cars, but the TF had one. In its erect position, the wiper blade sat along the bottom of the screen, and there was a rubber flap to keep draughts out of the base of the cockpit ...

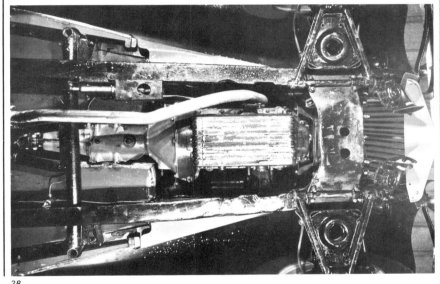

28

29

30

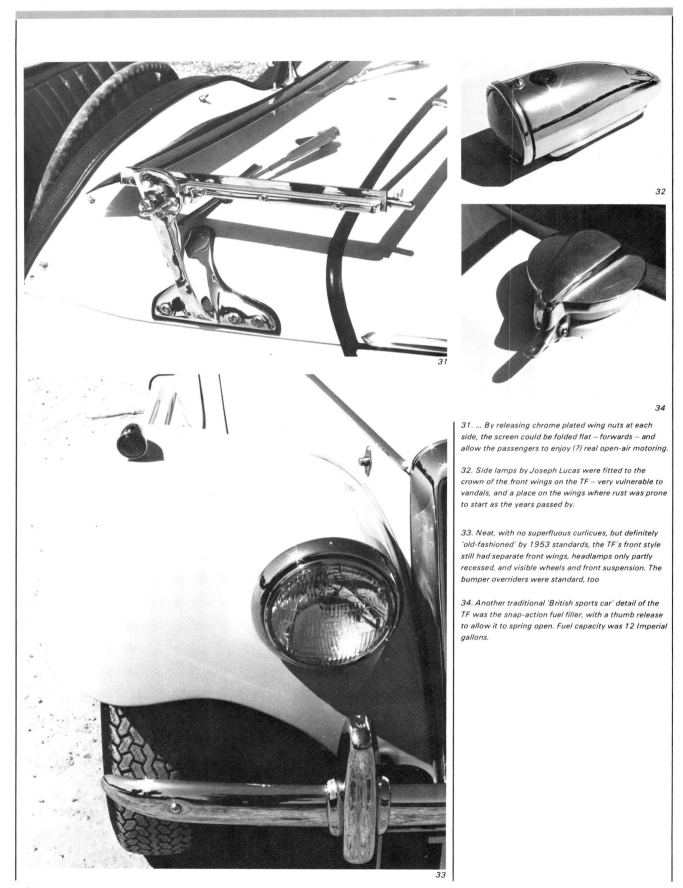

31. ... By releasing chrome plated wing nuts at each side, the screen could be folded flat – forwards – and allow the passengers to enjoy (?) real open-air motoring.

32. Side lamps by Joseph Lucas were fitted to the crown of the front wings on the TF – very vulnerable to vandals, and a place on the wings where rust was prone to start as the years passed by.

33. Neat, with no superfluous curlicues, but definitely 'old-fashioned' by 1953 standards, the TF's front style still had separate front wings, headlamps only partly recessed, and visible wheels and front suspension. The bumper overriders were standard, too

34. Another traditional 'British sports car' detail of the TF was the snap-action fuel filler, with a thumb release to allow it to spring open. Fuel capacity was 12 Imperial gallons.

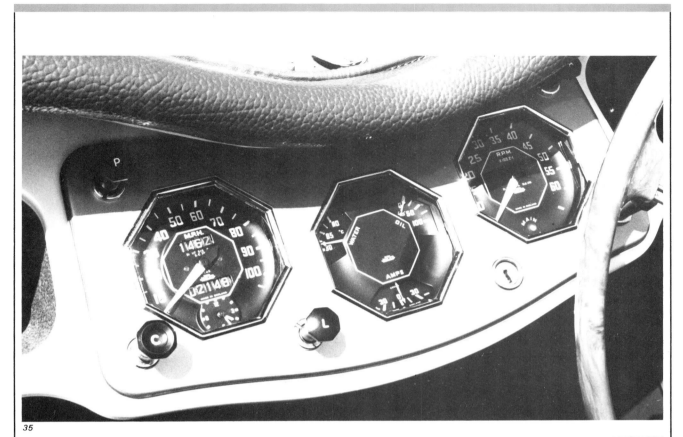

35

36

35. A close-up study of a TF instrument display. As this is not a 1950s picture, the mileage recorded – 2,148 – is not likely to be the total covered in the last 30 years! Note that there was no fuel contents gauge – you had to guess, or hand-carve a dip stick for the tank itself!

36. MG tradition, mixed in places with Nuffield modernisation and cost-savings. The octagonal instrument shapes speak for themselves, as do the positions of the horn and the direction indicator switches (by the driver's right hand), but the steering wheel had a rather horrid plastic rim.

37

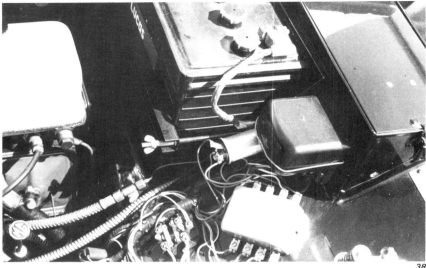

38

39

40

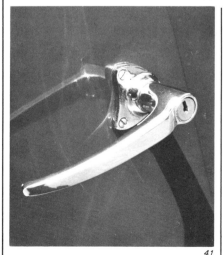

41

37. On the TF, there is, naturally, an octagon-shaped MG badge, and an octagon-shaped radiator filler cap — except that the filler cap is a dummy. The real filler cap is hidden under the bonnet, accessible from the left-hand side.

38. BMC/MG made no attempt to tidy up the under bonnet electrical wiring, although most of the fittings were concentrated on the left-hand side. The battery was in a cradle on the engine side of the bulkhead, with the toolbox behind it, and most electrical fittings — regulator, fuses and other small items — close by.

39. A bonnet with a central hinge, and fixed engine bay sides meant that access to the engine was restricted. The carburettors and their simple flame-trap air cleaners dominate the right-hand side opening.

40. The central bonnet hinge pin is easily unpicked from the main structure, when it exposes the top of the XPAG engine. Note the neat way in which air cleaners are angled to fit inside the confines of the space, to line up with the bonnet sides.

41. The TF's door handles dropped towards the rear when the doors were closed, not standing parallel to the ground.

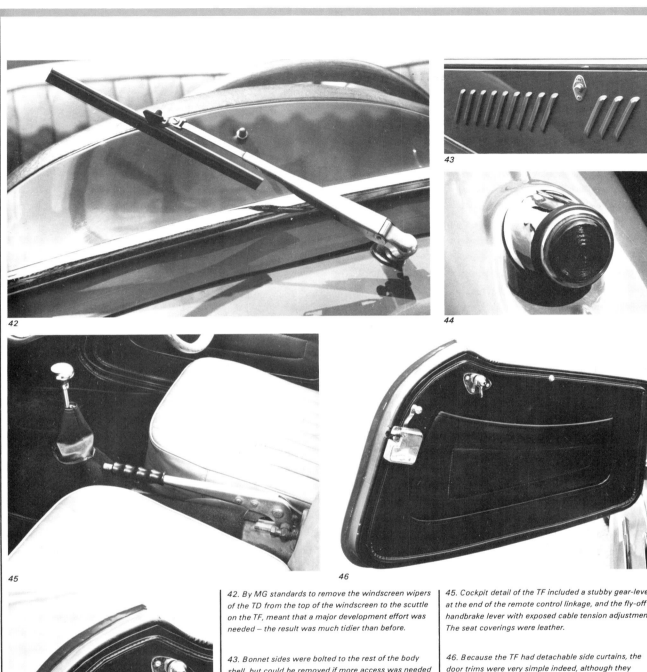

42. By MG standards to remove the windscreen wipers of the TD from the top of the windscreen to the scuttle on the TF, meant that a major development effort was needed – the result was much tidier than before.

43. Bonnet sides were bolted to the rest of the body shell, but could be removed if more access was needed to the engine. Louvres are to allow hot air to escape, while the push button was to release the fold-up top panels, which were not normally lockable.

44. Straight out of Joseph Lucas's parts bin were the stop/tail/direction indicator lamps fitted to the TF's rear wings. For all markets, of course, these had red plastic lenses.

45. Cockpit detail of the TF included a stubby gear-lever at the end of the remote control linkage, and the fly-off handbrake lever with exposed cable tension adjustment. The seat coverings were leather.

46. Because the TF had detachable side curtains, the door trims were very simple indeed, although they included spacious map pockets for stowage.

47. TF door furniture – including simple door locks, and fixings for the side-curtains, which had to be tightened up to keep them in place.

48

49

50

48. Most TF owners liked to run with their cars as open as possible, but in very cold and showery conditions they might erect the side curtains, if not the hood. These would normally be stored in the well behind the seats. The door curtains included flaps allowing a driver to make hand signals if he felt like it!

49. A nicely-preserved, high-mileage, TF, standard except for the steering wheel, which should have sprung wire spokes and a plastic rim.

50. The tonneau cover found on many TFs was often deployed like this, covering in the empty passenger seat area, but allowing the driver his open-air motoring.

51. Erecting the hood, which normally lived, in its stowed position, at the back of the well behind the seats.

52. With hood erect and side screens in place, the TF could be a surprisingly snug little car.

53. Tail view of the TF, typical of so many classic MGs, showing the ample ground clearance and — on this car — the optional wire wheels, and the accessory reflectors fixed to the bumper.

54. Just by looking at this picture you can see the joy of owning a TF — if, that is, the weather is favourable. Small, neat, and cobby — the TF's nimble handling was its nicest feature.

51

52

53

54

55

56

58

55. The TF was not used much by BMC in competitions, but Marcus Chambers's department used this example, KRX 90, for Pat Moss during 1955.

56. Each side of the bonnet top was released by depressing two button pushes. The sides could only be removed by unbolting them from the main structure.

57. The TF's 'trade-mark' included semi-faired headlamps, and a sloping-back radiator grille. The functional cooling radiator, incidentally, is hidden away behind the chrome grille. Note that there is still provision for a starting handle to be inserted through the front bumper.

58. Partly stowed and battened down hood and linkage, with the fuel tank behind it. There wasn't really space for anything other than luggage behind the front seats.

57

59. The tonneau completely deployed, with – as usual – a long central zip allowing only part of it to be furled if necessary.

60. As was normal with so many British cars of the period, 'Lift the Dot' fasteners were used for the fixing of the tonneau cover to the body shell.

61. Nothing garish, but everything functional, on the MG TF of 1953-1955. Many TF owners also added extra driving lamps (fixing them to the bumper irons to each side of the grille), and rear-view mirrors to the front wings.

59

60

61

62

63

62. Which is the most attractive aspect of the TF? Many would say it is this one, in which the rakish, though traditional, lines, are shown off so well. The TF must have been one of the last new cars to have running boards.

63. The TF as many of us like to remember it – square shouldered, squat, and ready for action, at any time, anywhere. Compared with the TD which it replaced, the TF's bonnet sloped down towards the nose, and the grille was angled back to blend with it.

64. Space in the TF for two, and luggage, but little else. Nowadays safety experts would be horrified by the use of rear-hinged doors, and by any car which did not have a roll-over safety hoop, but in the 1950s, buyers seemed not to worry about such things.

64

C1

C2

C1 & C2. Metamorphosis. The immediate post-war model, the TC, so very similar to the pre-war Midgets, was subtly changed to become the fuller, more rounded TD model, equipped with IFS.

49

C3

C3. Transformation complete. The TF.

C4. Old-style house, old-style car - a perfect setting for the Olde Englishe TF?

C5. Can you see the join? The TF's centre section was almost pure TD, but the sloping nose and more flared tail were new.

C4

C5

C6

C7

C6 & C7. Take off the centre bonnet hinge pin, remove both leaves of the bonnet, and most of the TF's engine is exposed. Note the position of the real radiator cap behind the dummy cap on the chrome grille.

C8. For the first time separate seats were fitted rather than the bench-back seats of all earlier standard T-Series models.

C9. Even though there was no space for rear passengers, the TF's seats could be tilted forward, presumably to make luggage loading easier.

C8

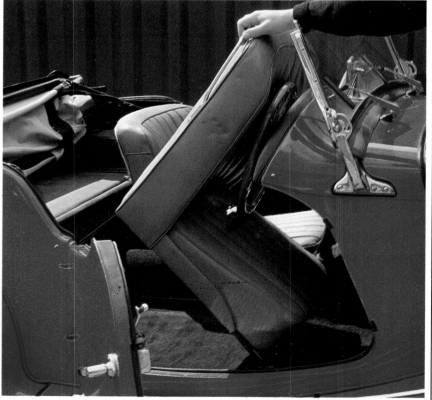

C9

C10

C11

SCV 730

C12

C13

C10. Front suspension detail. Even this, with trunnions rather than ball joints was a 'traditional' feature of the TF.

C11. The perforated disc wheels, introduced for the TD, were carried on, unchanged, for the TF ...

C12. ... although the centre-lock cap wire wheel remained an option.

C13. The TF was built for less than two years - 1953 to 1955 - and only 9,600 were made. Apart from the choice of wire or steel wheels, they all looked like this.

C14. The classic MG radiator grille style, which passed ample cooling air, so overheating was never a problem.

C15. Even on the facia, the TF had a lot of opportunity to show off its octagons, including the discreet badge on the passenger's side.

C16. The plastic rimmed steering wheel and octagonal instruments were very much of the style of the time.

C17. Hot day, clear skies, a TF1250 with the hood down and stowed. All you need now is a congenial companion, a romantic destination to drive for.

C18

C18. A magnificently preserved TF, not only with immaculate cream body metal, but splendid chrome bumpers and fittings. Beats black plastic, doesn't it?

C19. The sweeping wings and the running boards clad a body shell built up on a wooden skeleton, as developed by British craftsmen so very many years ago. On the TF, it would have looked right in the 1940s, but by the mid-1950s it was all beginning to look a bit old-fashioned.

C19

C20. One of a number of fine models available of the MGTF.

C21. The MGA; at once predecessor to and successor of the MGTF.

C20

C21